This book belongs to...

_____

and I am going to make the world better by doing ......

_____

This book is dedicated to the lovely "Mcflemster family" cousins,
who, like Nutty Nanny on a busy day, can be found all around the world.

Polly & Penny in Australia
Jesse in Abu Dhabi
Jess, Noah & Ezra in South Africa
and
Kit, Jesse & Casper 'up north'.
Phoebe & Freddie 'down south'
Larrie, Mollie & Lois 'in the middle'
of Britain.

May you each 'fly high' and make your own mark on the world!

# Nutty Nanny changes the World!

Illustrations and story by Debbie Flenley.

# Meet Nutty Nanny.....

She tells her grandchildren ....

You should always try to make the **worlD a better place**

Maybe for **You** it's by being kind – or – even, just picking up some litter.....

But **Nanny's Way** of doing it is ....

(you'll never guess??)

She has only gone and made herself an AEROPLANE !!!

Oh Nanny!!!

"I am going off to see the **greatest** things in the world," she said, "and make them **even GREATER!**"

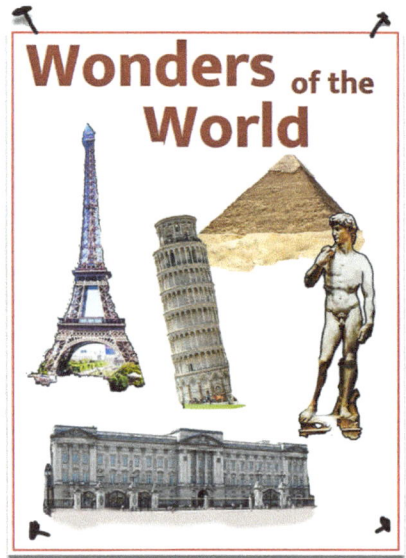

Oh Dear!... This is never going to end well!

First of all,
Nanny went to Florence, in Italy
and visted the Statue of David.
(carved out of marble by Michelangelo the Artist)

"Well GooDness GraCious Gravy!" she gasped.
"He's got no PANTS"
Thats too ruDe !

We will have to see what we can do about **THAT!**

The next morning, the poor Museum Guard got a right old **shock!!!**

**"great GallopinG Greeny pants"** he cried,

"what on earth has happened here?"

**"Nutty nanny DiD it,"** said Dave the statue,

and so,....that **1** guard chased after her......

......But Nan just ran, onto her next plan.....

Nanny stayed in Italy and saw the **leaning Tower in Piza.**

( Because it was built on soft land, over the years, it had started to lean)

"**Well Goodness Gracious Gravy!**" she gasped.

**That's too Dangerous!!**

We will have to see what we can do about **THAT!**

The next morning, the tower guard got a right old shock!!!
"Tumbling towers and tortellini!!" she cried
"what on earth has happened here?"

"Nutty nanny did it,"
said the tourists,

and so, .....now
2 Guards chased after her

But Nan just ran onto her next plan.....

Nutty Nanny then went to Egypt and saw **the PyramiDs.**

(They were built hundreds of years ago to put the dead bodies of their important Pharaohs in.)

**"Well GooDness GraCious Gravy!"** she gasped.

"There's no windows!

**That's too Dark!!**"

"We will have to see what we can do about **THAT!**"

Nutty Nanny then went to Paris in France.
and saw **the Eiffel tower**

(It was built over 130 years ago for a big fair
and it has 1,665 steps!!)

"**Well Goodness Gracious Gravy!**" she gasped.

"There's no rides!"

**That's too boring!!**"

We will have to see what we can do about **THAT!**"

The next morning the Tower Guard was in for a right old **shock!**

"**Freaky froGs leGs**' he cried

"What on earth has happened here?"

weeeeeee
"**Nanny DiD it!**" said the roller coaster riders,
Weeeeeeeee

and so .....now
**4 GuarDs** chased after her....

....But Nan just ran onto her next plan......

Finally, Nanny went home to London in Britain to see **Buckingham Palace** where the King and Queen officially live.

(It has 52 bedrooms for guests and 78!!!! toilets and even a secret swimming pool)

"**Well Goodness Gracious Gravy!**" she gasped.

All for just for two people!

**That's too biG!!**"

We will have to see what we can do about **THAT!!**

Then....
SUDDENLY
...Nanny saw the Guards all following her

"OOOPs" thought Nutty Nanny,
"looks like I'm in trouble

BiG Trouble !!"

She didn't know what to do,
so she
found somewhere to

HidE!!

They said to her,
## "We think what you have Done is GREAT!"

The Statue is not so **RudE** now!
The Leaning Tower is not so **DANGEROUS** now!
The Pyramid is not so **DARK** now!
The Eiffel Tower is not so **BORING** now!

**anD, some one very special Wants to tell you Nanny, that the Great biG palace ...."**

**anD...**

Nanny was given a big shiny **meDal** because it is important to make the world a better place

# Well done Nanny !

**THE ENd**

Now, what can YOU do, to make YOUR world better ?

# How I could change my world .....

## General ideas

- Make a little gift for an old person in your street
- Help at home – ask if there are any jobs that need doing.
- Give some of your pocket money to a charity
- Raise some money for a charity ( sell lemonade or cakes or your toys?)
- Find out about Global warming or endangered animals. ... then .....
- Raise awareness; (Tell your classmates and friends what you have found out)
- Support someone at school who seems to be sad (– or needs a friend )
- Pick up some litter
- Plants some flowers from some seeds
- Pat a dog ( ask first !)

ALWAYS CHECK WITH A GROWN UP BEFORE YOU DO THESE ...

## Your ideas

Now, make a list of your ideas – things you could do to make the world around you better

**(Keep this list for future reference)**

- 
- 
- 
- 
- 
- 
- 
- 
-

# HoW Do you think you coulD make your WorlD a better place?

It doesn't have to be a big thing, like Nutty Nanny did

( in fact it's best if you never touch famous monuments!! )

**Maybe, it coulD be....**

**a GooD DeeD you Do, somethinG you tiDy up, Or improve, or someone you help?**

**DraW a piCture of What it Was like BEFORE you ChanGeD thinGs**

*You Can Do it, just like i DiD*

now ....

**draW a piCture of What it Was like AFTER you maDe the ChanGes!**

# Organisations to help children make the world a better place.

If you want to help make your world a better place, these groups have children's sections and can give you information, kids groups to join, and fun things to do.

National geographic kids ( natgeokids.com)

Young people's trust for the environment ( ypte.org.uk)

Kids against plastic - KAP ( kidsagainstplastic.co.uk)

World land trust  ( worldlandtrust..org)

Friends of the earth  (friendsoftheearth.co.uk)

Defenders of the planet ( kidsforsavingearth.org)

# The Nutty Nanny series

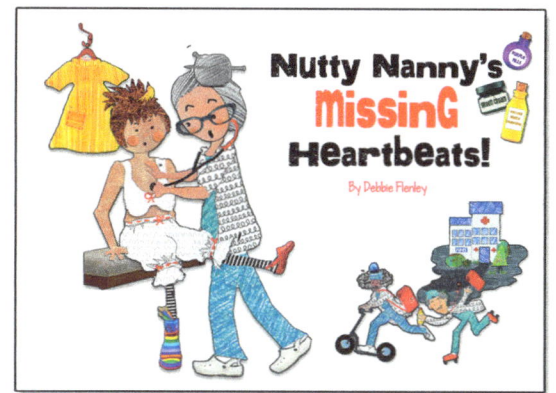

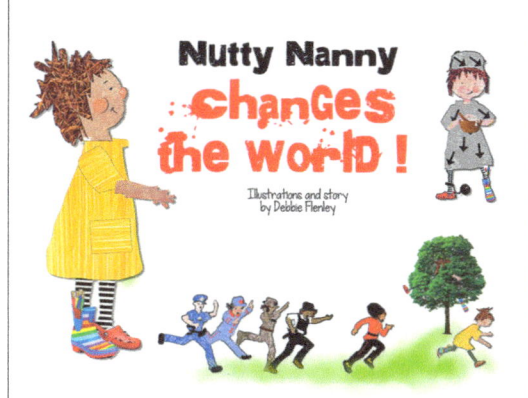

Debbie Flenley draws on her experience as a Teacher & Grandma to help children think about life issues....

including......

Living apart from a loved one,
(Nanny's missing heart beat)

Overcoming obstacles to achieve your dream.
(Nanny's Space adventure)

Making your impact on the world
( Nanny changes the world)

These delightful stories include lots of talking points and "funnies" to keep children engaged and challenged

Enjoy, laugh and discuss ...maybe.... self belief, love, perseverance, dreams and and how to 'think outside the box' Nanny style !

www.debbieflenley.co.uk
Debbieflenley58@gmail.com

www.ingramcontent.com/pod-product-compliance
Lightning Source LLC
Chambersburg PA
CBHW050855010526
44118CB00004BA/172